7 Life Lessons on the Myths of Marriage

7 Life Lessons on the Myths of Marriage

Abu Layth

Published by CreateSpace

Produced by Live to Inspire Publishers
A Division of the Abu Layth Life Lessons Group
www.abulayth.com

© Copyright Abu Layth 2016

7 LIFE LESSONS ON THE MYTHS OF MARRIAGE

ISBN 978-0-9935095-0-6

Live to Inspire Publishers are trademarks of the
Abu Layth Life Lessons Group.
Designed by Abu Layth
Manufactured in the United Kingdom

Book formatted by www.bookformatting.co.uk.

Contents

Author's Note to Readers

All views held in this book are based upon personal experience and observation of the author. The content is designed to assist and support individuals however; it is not guaranteed to provide the stated results for all readers.

This book is sold with the understanding that it is to be utilised as a tool towards building a healthy marriage and by no means is it meant as a sole-solution towards attaining that result.

Is It All Make Believe?

When did marriage become so sensationalised? When did the true essence of this beautiful bond become lost within misconceptions of what we now misunderstand matrimony to be?

Marriage is not the myths that we have begun to believe – marriage is coexistence far more raw and intrusive than we choose to accept. *7 Life Lessons on the Myths of Marriage*™ will challenge these common flawed understandings that society as a whole seems to have embraced. This book seeks to realign our understanding of marriage so that we can enjoy a healthier and happier marital existence, or simply allow us to be better placed in understanding the challenges of marriage before entering into the sacred bond, thereby better preparing us for what should be the most worthwhile struggle of our lives.

When we look at the bare facts, it is more than evident that marriages are suffering significantly. Statistics looking at divorce in England and Wales in 2012 showed that there were 13 divorces *every hour* for that year alone, with 1 in 7 divorces being granted on the grounds of adultery. The shocking truth does not end there – it has been projected that almost 50% of marriages will inevitably end in divorce. Another such study revealed that 60% of married couples were unhappy in their marriage, and 40% considered leaving their partner as a result. This is not a trend that is limited to just one part of society or a particular ethnic group – no, this is a worldwide issue, and it is becoming increasingly apparent in the Muslim world –though we once boasted an almost unconditional honouring of marriage.

There seems to be many painful trends that feature recurrently within broken or weak marriages, these include a lack of sexual satisfaction by both parties, lack of compatibility, different life goals, breakdown of trust and adultery – to mention but a few. This book intends to tackle these very issues and provide solutions to those suffering as a result of marriage, but first, we need to understand why things have changed so dramatically in recent years.

When we look at ourselves within the context of today's world, we know that our environment and our challenges are far different in comparison to those generations that saw the birth of Islam, in all honesty, we do not even have to draw such a stark comparison – if we go back just 50 years we know that our social climates have changed vastly.

Is it any wonder that marriage is misunderstood within an increasingly hypersexualised society? Is it any wonder that marriage is dishonoured when we as a community no longer understand the word honour? Does it come as anything but a surprise to know that materialism dictates much of our life goals, and with that, morality seems to have got lost; so how can such a world expect to hold fast to the concept of marriage?

It is no longer just a "Western" problem. With liberal concepts seeping into every community through various forms of media outlets, whether it be Facebook or satellite TV – we are all ultra-exposed to false-realities at the click of a button, and the damage that these false-realities are leaving, are truly devastating. As a society, we are becoming increasingly dissociated from real interaction, and we are becoming absorbed in a virtual world in order to escape the unbearable misery of our current life. Happiness has become a concept that we now associate with TV sitcoms, or it is found in chasing hollow worldly dreams.

The fact is this is not how things have to be.

Marriage is a promise between two individuals, it is a trust that has been enjoined between two loving souls, and it is a bond within which both Love and Mercy are meant to grow.

"...He Created for you mates from among yourselves that ye may dwell in tranquility with them, and He has put love and mercy between your (hearts)..."
[Surah Ar Rum, 30: part of verse 21]

Marriage can be reclaimed, it can be everything that it should be, and so much more, all that is required is for us to abolish these myths from our mind, and *truly* understand the sanctimony of this sacred vow once again.

So how can this be done?

Without doubt, there is a significant need for education within our communities from an early age on the stark realities of marriage; we cannot allow our future generations to learn about an act which completes half of one's religion via social media and television, all of which is geared towards a liberalised culture and holds little value or worth in the Islamic context. It is this very hope that I aim to at least initiate within this book; I refuse to remain a casual observer of this devastating trend – I stand firm in the hope of reviving the forgotten essence of marriage, and seek to set our future generations in better stead than we may have seen. Furthermore, I am confident that regardless of where your own marriage may be at this current time, this book can assist you in gaining greater clarity in regaining happiness once more.

You may question my expertise in this area however, I have spent years advising and supporting individuals through a range of marital issues; from affairs to sexual dissatisfaction, to mental and physical abuse and even as far as prostitution – I have seen much of the issues that are painfully seeping into our homes, and I can no longer remain silent on that which breaks my heart. Having suffered the pains of divorce myself, I am well versed on the downfalls that are created through misconceiving marriage.

It is more than possible for us to reclaim the peace and ease that we all would have sought when entering into marriage, and as you progress through this book, you will begin to learn about the myths that can potentially devastate the state of your relationship. As I teach you about these myths, I will also equip you with the means to dispel these delusions and begin to re-evaluate the true nature of your relationship, and begin to find a deeper sense of peace once again.

7 Life Lessons on the Myths of Marriage™ will explore fully the most common misconceptions individuals hold prior to entering into marriage. These have been compiled based upon the vast experiences that I have gained from advising couples who are dealing with a variety of issues, through which common trends became apparent. It seems that the majority of us become so accustomed to our unhappy states that we give up on seeking to rekindle the joy that we once knew, and in many cases, we enter into marriage with a multitude of false notions that inevitably set us up for devastation.

I am excited to be exploring this topic in-depth, and serving you with the opportunity to realise a happier relationship state.

"When you are attracted to someone's physical beauty, their impact fades with time. When your heart is touched by the beauty of someone's soul, then know their impact echoes through your entire life."

CHAPTER 1:

How Did This Come To Be?

There is no denying the facts – they speak clearly of the unhappy reality; marriages are not lasting – they are no longer weathering the storm with the perseverance that was once shown.

Why?

The problems are multi-faceted and they are corroding the family structure before it is even formed.

In order to fully appreciate the problems, we need to take a step back and evaluate where the weaknesses first become apparent.

If we look at our parents, and the generation that preceded them, we learn a lot about ourselves, and what we have subsequently lost. Primarily, from one generation to the next, there is a loss of understanding the true importance of values. It is clear to see that the principles that our parents hold firmly to, we struggle to fully comprehend. To give just one example, our ability to tolerate imperfection is something that has become almost unknown. We are so accustomed to getting the most up-to-date gadgets, our desire to tolerate anything but the "best" is almost non-existent, whereas if we look to our parents, we see a generation of individuals who grafted with little to their name, in the mere hope of developing foundations upon which their families could prosper. They were a generation willing to possess nothing, in the hope that their future generations would possess so much more. They learnt the concept of sacrifice, and by Allah, they lived that sacrifice with excellence. That is not to say that we are a generation completely free of this concept however, we have gained home comforts with lesser struggles, thereby

1

leaving us less willing to give up the comforts we have come to know.

Furthermore, when we look to the attitude that has been bred within our earlier generations, there seemed to be a very adamant mind set, giving up was not a term that featured in their vocabulary, and certainly not in terms of marriage! This can have positive and negative aspects drawn from it. The negative essentially being that even when people were legitimately unhappy within their relationships, they were unable to escape such situations, therefore suffering though our Deen (faith) does not make this incumbent upon us. The more positive aspect from this mind-set is fairly apparent – when we are unwilling to give up, we do what many folk fail to do today, and that is simply to exhaust every avenue that may salvage the marital commitment that was once made, and so hoping to fulfil the promise of making marriage lifelong.

Increasingly, we have become a society more concerned with the shortfalls of others and less concerned with bettering ourselves. Naturally, in a marital situation, we will be paired with someone who appears perfect from the outset but in reality, our logical side knows that there is no true perfection in this life - perfection is simply a state we strive for, but never fully achieve. In marriage, perfection is a concept that means the acceptance of one's spouse despite their imperfections. How then can marriages survive when we cannot tolerate the less-than perfect individuals we find ourselves waking up next to?

To add to our psychological barriers, today's world has exposed us to unrealistic ideologies with respect to the male and female physical forms, with flawless bodies appearing in every possible media outlet, forcing such ridiculous concepts of what our spouses should look like, dress like, and behave like. How can such images serve as healthy food for our thoughts?

In addition to this, the media industries are becoming increasingly hyper-sexualised with nudity and eroticism being used as bait for most marketing tools. Beyond just marketing, we find that most television sitcoms are laced with innuendo, and most are now so explicit in their sexual content that we have no healthy escape through such means.

When we look at the generation around us who may have grown up watching various series including *Friends, Sex and the City* and *ER* to name but a few, it is safe to say that our understanding of relationships and love will have been poisoned to some extent by the content of these shows. Each of these shows project a hyper-liberal concept about relationships and intimacy – so how can we as a society exposed to such things remain grounded and true to our conservative principles?

There is no denying that today's world has begun to plant seeds of corruption against the purity that marriage is supposed to encourage, and from this, our misconceptions of marriage have come to grow.

As we progress through the following chapters, I intend to realign our thoughts regarding marriage by redirecting our misunderstandings rooted to societal and psychological concepts, and offering the solutions towards dispelling those very myths that appear to be destroying matrimonial allegiances.

"Hope often enters our lives dressed as disaster."

CHAPTER 2:

What Do I know?

Everyone will have their opinions on the topic of marriage, but there are few who have endured it, and learnt from it. The vast majority of us simply find ourselves in a state of unhappiness, and accepting it, because what else is there to do?

My story is different. It is mine, and it has taught me what I share with you now. Ironically, it is only through failure that we learn of how we can succeed, and when it came to marriage, that was exactly what I had to do.

I failed, miserably, but I refused to stop there. I refused to let failure define who I would become. I got it completely wrong, but then through that, I also took a step back, and looked for where I got so lost, and so sought to ensure that wherever possible, I helped others avoid similar downfalls.

I have always been a community man; active in seeing the youth prosper and being involved with local issues. However, I never anticipated becoming an advisor to many of the fragments of our community, both online and offline.

Having served in Strathclyde Police, I also found myself inadvertently working as a mediator in a number of familial issues ranging from the youth becoming derailed, Muslims getting involved in drugs and improper conduct, and marital discord. It was through this route that I found myself becoming increasingly pulled upon in assisting others through their own marital breakdowns. Ironic some may say, but a blessing nonetheless. With that said, I knew that I had something to offer, I knew that my own experiences had formed me and had taught me vital life lessons that could only benefit these people crying out for help. So I embraced the challenge, and stepped onto a path that has led me here, today, speaking to you about this very topic, Alhamdulillah.

When I first married, I was young, and hasty; everything was done, simply for the sake of doing. Little thought went into the process, I went on instant whims and hoped for the best results, never fully appreciating that each action required effort, and each action came with consequences. Looking back, I realise how immature a young man I was, and how foolish my outlook on life had been, but Alhamdulillah; to stand tall, we must first fall, and know what the world looks like from a lower perspective.

Needless to say, my marriage served me with many difficult lessons, it butchered the naivety that got me into that painful predicament, and fiercely taught me how to become the man that I am now. My marriage did not endure the distance however; it has provided me the path towards a better existence.

Having become a wounded divorcee, I found many people instantly drawn to me when seeking help in their own marital ups and downs; I began to see very clear and apparent patterns in all these cases. Through the years, I have advised and mediated for, a vast array of couples, most of whom I have assisted in finding their areas of contention, and putting them to rest, and a few, who have mutually come to realise that marriage between them was no longer a realistic nor happy route.

Each case has taught me something more in the matter of marriage, and it has allowed me even more firmness and faith in pursuing this objective.

To share just two case scenarios, each on the opposite end of the spectrum to the other. The first, they were a young couple of subcontinent origin; clearly newlywed, and clearly very content. I often looked at them and wondered what created this peace between them. They seemed to just be at ease around one another – almost like they were enveloped in patience. I happened to come across them whilst lunching, and I saw the wife, feeding her husband from her plate, from her own hands, before her own self; I saw sacrifice, and a happy and willing one at that.

The second, as mentioned, were the complete opposite to the first. Being in there company instantly brought unease; you felt the tension in the air; it seemed that each word that was uttered between them was laced with bitterness and resentment – I couldn't understand how two individuals who would have known each other so intimately, came to hate each other so intently? As time passed, I realised that what lay between them was false expectations. They had begun a journey with their individual ideals of what married life would be, and as they walked these paths, they found themselves increasingly divergent from one another. They began to blame one another for unfulfilled hopes and dreams; their marriage became a source of distress and unhappiness.

Having seen this and so much more, I began to compile detailed analysis of where things seemed to go wrong, looking for those common threads that if unwoven, they see the unraveling of marriage beyond repair.

I have made this book my hope in sharing wisdoms on how to prevent you from stumbling into these common pitfalls, and providing you tried and tested methods by which you can ensure your mind bears a healthy ideal of what marriage truly is.

Love is raw; it takes effort, commitment & selflessness.

CHAPTER 3:

All is Not Lost

Without doubt, the struggle within marriage is real but I can quite honestly say a lot of the struggle is due to what is cultivated within our minds prior to us even entering marriage.

The soil that is soft, and tender, is more likely to absorb water, and through that it becomes healthier, allowing for much benefit to come. However, the land which is hard and dry, it is filled with cracks; the water generally passes over it, or is held only on the surface of it; that land will not yield anything healthy. And so too, can we liken this analogy to the human mind; the soil that is soft is the mind that is open and susceptible to the realities that its situation will bring, it is a mind that is prepared to face the challenges that lie ahead without being impermeable to the conditions it endures. The hard soil can be likened to the mind that is unaware of flexibility, of sacrifice and hardship; it is a mind that has been polluted by myths and misconceptions, and so is shackled to falsehood, and simply cracks and rejects, when faced with the realities of life.

So where does hope lie? Hope lies in our understanding ourselves better.

Marriage is a journey of two individuals; each of whom submits to the other in a promise stated in the most simplistic of terms: "I will help you along". So, when we look at this rather basic statement of marriage, what is striking about it is that in order to help someone else, we must first and foremost, be in a position of strength within our own selves. It is this very concept that lays the foundation of much of my Life Lessons within this book.

We expect marriage to be the means by which we are miraculously healed through coexistence with another person. Sadly, that is one of many myths that lead to an unhealthy mind prior to marriage.

The solution lies within you. You are the source to the healthy and happy marital state that you seek. You are the means by which things can be changed. Within you, lies hope.

Too many of us have falsified this notion of marriage through our over-exposure to a non-committal ideology. Alhamdulillah, marriage does serve as a source of love and mercy, as is the Promise of Allah, Most High. However, before that can be attained, we must appreciate fully its primary objective. As with everything in the life of a believer, our primary purpose lies in the worship of Allah. This is the sole reason for our creation.

"We have Created Jinn and mankind only that they might worship Me."
[Adh-Dhariyat, 51: verse 56]

Now let that sink in for a moment. You and I would not be here, we would not be in existence, had it not been for Allah wishing for us to worship Him, and Him Alone. That's pretty deep, and more than that, that makes us pretty special. We exist because He Chose us to exist, furthermore, we exist, because He wished for us to worship Him, Alhamdulillah.

So now, you might be thinking, what does that have to do with marriage? Well, I can say with absolute conviction, it has everything to do with marriage. Allah, by His Mercy and Wisdom created marriage as a source of companionship, through which we can fulfil some of our most base desires, and more than that; a means by which we are increased in our worship of Him.

Marriage is a beautiful form of worship when done correctly, but when it is done wrongly, it opens the path to sin upon sin.

It is with the amalgamation of these two foundational concepts that my framework for *7 Life Lessons on the Myths of Marriage*™ has come to be.

A healthy-self with a healthy understanding of marriage, in its truest and most real sense, (i.e. that which is taught within the Qur'an and Sunnah) is the solid foundation that is required in order to build a secure and enduring life with your spouse.

At this moment, I want you to just pause.

Am I right in thinking that your instant response is: "I've heard all this already"?

You're right, you probably have, but then, let me ask you this, why did you pick up this book?

Though you know the facts, how much of it has been successfully implemented into your current life? I was once in that exact same situation; constantly in pursuit of answers, constantly seeking advice, and absorbing knowledge from wherever I could find it. I knew a lot. What became clear with time was that though I had the knowledge, I didn't put much of it into practice hence my situation remaining stagnant.

This is where I challenge you to continue reading. My promise is simple; I will provide you with the tools that will open your mind to a healthier spiritual and emotional state, through which you will attain a healthier and happier outlook upon your marriage. I need only one thing from you, and that is to leave your skepticism to the side; strip your mind of the weeds that naturally poison the soil of our souls, and get ready to plant seeds towards a happier you, and a far more blissful marriage.

CHAPTER 4:

Myth no. 1 – Honeymoon Lusts are an Eternal Bliss

Pre-marriage, there's this lust-fuelled, hormonal frenzy that overcomes all forms of logic. In some cases, this can be so intense that it masks even the most glaringly apparent incompatibilities between individuals. Amongst even the more mature and level-headed of individuals, it would seem that we are all mildly guilty of allowing our hearts to dance into a rather unrealistic idea of what married reality has in-store.

From personal experience, the nature of this myth varies depending on the nature of the "afflicted" individual.

If we look at the majority of our youth, and if we look at the nature of what they are exposed to via TV and Film, it is quite clear to see that their understanding of relationships is heavily influenced by a very sexually explicit ideology.

So what exactly does that entail?

Put simply; boy meets girl, there appears to be a mutual inclination towards one another, they become friends; the text flirting begins, things become exciting because there's heightened emotional intensity with each flirtatious exchange. They begin to date; physically being in one another's company – the intensity grows, and the intimacy begins to unfold; first with the holding of hands, and the longing-gazes into one another's eyes, and then naturally, lust gives way – kissing seems almost impossible to avoid. Once one door of intimacy opens, it inevitably leads to a fumbling towards the next.

Where does it stop – or does it stop at all?

As much as the reality is bitter and rather difficult to swallow; it is our reality. This may be the actual lifestyle that much of our youth have now adopted, or may be their ingrained understanding of what relationships should play out like.

If we assume the best, and presume that this is just the mind set of our youth, then we need to look at what that means for them and their understanding of marriage.

To begin with, this whole Hollywood and Bollywood concept of relationships is modelled around an exaggerated emphasis on the physical aspects of male-female interactions. How would one expect to attain sky-high viewing figures for a sitcom if it showed the day-to-day norms of a relationship? There is no drama in watching two people talk about what groceries need to be bought in for the week, or whose turn it is to take the rubbish out? In other words; sex sells, and sadly, sex has sold the sense of many of our youth for a very cheap price!

When we are constantly exposed to heated physical interactions being the norms between men and women, it is only natural that we start using these as a measure by which we then go on to gauge our own expectations.

In addition, most commonly, our youth are faced with two very disparate concepts of relationships; on one hand there is this hyper-sexualised idea and the other being their own parent's relationship – usually a hyper-conservative situation where there is little, to no sign of any emotional attachment. This creates a very dangerous situation in young impressionable minds, especially when two very different messages are being portrayed. All too often, when looking to our parents and their marriages there can be an assumption of "two people just getting by", and when this is compared to the excitement of two "in love" individuals, there is no wonder the youth are inclined to seek the latter of the options.

The problem arises when such thoughts are allowed to formulate and become the benchmarks to our reality; to believe that life with another person are moments of flirtatious exchanges that open the way to kisses at every-given opportunity, followed by nights of endless intimacy – that is a dangerous concept to be reliant upon.

Marriage is not that, but it can become something far more beautiful than that.

If we allow one's lust to determine their choice in future spouse, the resultant outcome is an inevitable dissipation of a relationship. It is not possible for a life-long commitment to be formed on such a superficial notion of sexual satisfaction alone; naturally once this has been fulfilled and routine sets in, it is only normal for one's desire for substantial companionship to start to formulate.

In essence, there is a real need for the differentiation between lust and true-attraction. Naturally, we do need to find the physicality of a potential partner appealing however, this needs to be understood within context of a life- long journey together; as cliché as it may sound, looks do fade, and it is the character of individuals that often become increasingly beautiful with the passing of time. Both aspects need to be balanced accordingly, and in order to confirm that it is not hormones that are driving your decision, prior to any pursuit of a potential partner; one must develop clear questions that would be posed, in order to ensure that maximal compatibility is achieved.

With that aside, it would seem that there are rather dark seeds sown in the minds of many regarding how marital bliss should be. From the outset, there is this unspoken matter of sexual intimacy; after all, marriage is the halal means by which this base desire is allowed to be explored and fulfilled within the limits set by Allah. However, this is a matter that is often completely unknown and completely misunderstood due to the community deeming it too shameful to speak of. This topic alone warrants a book of its own and so I will only touch the surface of this subject in this context.

Marital bliss in the eyes of so many young individuals quite simply equates to sexual bliss. So when we look at this from another perspective, if the sexual experience does not meet the expectations of the two individuals, then marital bliss has automatically become fragmented. If there was no emphasis put on the different areas of compatibility, then this one area of weakness can lead to a gradual dissolving of the relationship.

In context of this myth, there seems to be an understanding amongst many newlyweds that the feelings, the excitement and the intensity that exists in the initial few months of marriage set the tone for the remainder of married life. It seems to be that our exposure to falsified concepts of marriage, eat into all of ours' minds with respect to this myth. To take but one example, I know of even the most "practicing" of Muslims who have understood the struggle that is embodied within marriage, but still find themselves holding overly romanticised concepts; long nights spent with the wife stroking her husband's beard whilst he softly recites Quran, with them only ever exchanging kind words and good manners with one another. As much as this is a beautiful and noble ideal that many of us would hope for, it is somewhat unrealistic, especially when one has never been in a situation where they are suddenly so intimately involved with another person in every aspect of their lives. So no matter our background or upbringing, each of us will have some sort of understanding of what we expect in marriage, and the extent to which this concept is close to reality, determines how one then goes on to face marriage itself.

In essence, the concept of Honeymoon Bliss is fantastic, and Alhamdulillah, for some it lasts for most part of the first year of marriage however, to expect that that is the tone for the remaining years of marriage is, in actual fact, an injustice to the whole purpose of marriage.

For a relationship to develop healthily it must be open to the impact of external forces; the two individuals must be prepared to face the challenges that life inevitably brings with unmoved determination. This cannot therefore happen when a couple remains in a bubble of bliss where there is this almost superficial relationship that exists, where neither partner is truly being themselves, and in order to sustain this "blissful" state, each of them continuously pretends that situations and issues are of no concern, when in reality, they are aware of problems, but out of fear of impacting this blissful status quo, no-one wishes to step forwards, and simply be honest.

Therefore, this honeymoon phase, if held onto too closely, can actually be damaging. It is unrealistic to go through life with another person without being true to yourself, without being honest, open and vulnerable before them. The honeymoon bliss is a lovely starting point, but it is during this point of soft hearts and heightened love that each partner should be seeking to lay the groundwork for how they wish to strengthen their relationship.

Know that the honeymoon period is vital and it allows one to be lulled into the demands of marriage, but only if utilised cleverly.

Most commonly, each partner wishes to ensure that there is no cause for fights or disruption to the loving environment that exists, and that is fair enough, but what I advise at this stage, is to speak softly of the issues that do begin to materialise even in the early stages of marriage.

To build upon an earlier point, this concept that sexual bliss equates to marital bliss – where one, or both partners have concerns regarding matters of intimacy within the relationship, it may be that neither wishes to, or more likely, knows how to approach the issue. Rather than allowing these incredibly important matters go unaddressed, it is vital that they are met head-on, and what better time than during the early months of marriage. At this stage, marriage is new to you both, and each of you is on a journey of learning about the needs of your partner. This is why honeymoon bliss is actually more about a journey of learning; a year that leads onto a lifetime of wishing to understand the person that you have committed yourself to.

Commonly, it is fear that leads to people wishing to hold onto this myth; no-one wants to face the harsh realities of marriage when they can remain in a bubble of love, kindness and ease. At this point, let me be frank; a relationship that remains stagnant allows for little growth, and the purpose of marriage is for two individuals to grow together, spiritually, emotionally and mentally, in the hope of attaining Jannah.

The best advice that I can offer to any married couple or soon-to-be married individual is that the first while of a well-chosen marriage is beautiful; it's fun and exciting, and it should be enjoyed, but amidst all of this, remember the end-goal. Do not forget why you have begun this journey, and do not forget that this journey will be littered with challenges. So start setting the way for that long journey, and pack the provisions needed in order to endure it with ease.

The initial months are perfect for talking to your partner. As mentioned earlier, we are all guilty of being a little starry eyed in the early stages, so talking about things is actually easier; most of us want to ensure that we are pleasing our partner, and so are more open to *well-delivered* observations and concerns. Do not shy away from saying how you feel but always take great care with the tone that you use, and the time at which to deliver the feedback. Our later chapters will speak about this in greater detail, in'shaa'Allah.

In addition, use the honeymoon period to observe your partner; start taking mental notes of their adorable qualities, and always have these in your mind. There will inevitably come times when satan will aim to enforce only a negative perception of your spouse in your mind – so be prepared, take note of all those great qualities, and carry those forwards in your marriage.

In retrospect, know that your partner will inevitably begin to demonstrate their flaws as well. We need to take great care when it comes to such matters; our Prophetic teachings address this point so beautifully:

> *"A believer must not hate a believing woman (i.e. his wife);*
> *if he dislikes one of her traits he will be pleased with another."*
> [Sahih Muslim]

This teaching is applicable to both partners; it is very easy for us to become hung up on the flaws of others and this is when it is important to truly appreciate our own flaws first and foremost. None of us is perfect, nor will we ever attain perfection, so it is vital that we do not develop an unrealistic expectation of others when we ourselves know we could not achieve that.

With respect to managing the flaws of our spouses, it is vital that we filter them through our minds:

- Does the flaw impact your marital lives significantly or is it just something that you are struggling to overlook?
- Has the flaw escalated over time, leading you to fear that if left unaddressed, it will just continue to spiral?
- Is your spouse aware of the problem and of the extent to which it bothers you?

The above basic filtration system allows you to determine whether the matter needs to be discussed, and to what extent. If it is just a matter that you are struggling to overlook, then you need to apply effort into looking beyond it; focus on the aspects of your spouse that you are content with. If it is a matter that is escalating, and impacts you heavily, then it does need to be tackled directly through sensitive discussion with your spouse.

Naturally, any festering issue between two people who live so closely together can become divisive if not addressed. Generally, I would touch upon the topics of flaws with utmost sensitivity and always contextualise them in a manner that demonstrates the genuine concern for the health of the marriage. When this is the focus of any conversation between two individuals, the resultant outcome is generally a positive and healthy one.

To summarise, the honeymoon period was never meant to last forever although, it does serve as a wonderful softener into marriage. When we use those early months to set the foundations for communication and addressing the joint objectives of marriage; the honeymoon period can serve as the best part of a healthy future together.

Life Lesson 1:

"From the early moments of love and embraces, let there be a determination to seek to grow together, to not be fooled into loving a moment, but for loving one another."

CHAPTER 5:

Myth no. 2 - Love Is All We Need

"Of Love - may God exalt you! The first part is jesting, and the last part is right earnestness. So majestic are its diverse aspects, they are too subtle to be described; their reality can only be apprehended by personal experience. Love is neither disapproved by Religion, nor prohibited by the Law; for every heart is in God's hands."

[Ibn Hazm]

Love is the obsession of every creature since the beginning of time. The above quote embodies the truths of love so succinctly; when we embark upon this journey of love, we enjoy the lightness of it, we are lost in the lust and frolics of it, but as it develops, love takes on an intensity and rawness that some of us fail to anticipate; it envelopes us and infiltrates every part of us, leaving us sick with its affliction and longing for it, when lost. Love teaches us truths about ourselves in a way no other emotion manages. Love leaves us vulnerable and open to the most beautiful, and at times, the most painful experiences of our lives. Ibn Hazm then goes on to describe that love is something that is natural to every creature and an emotion that is not always a willing choice; who our hearts become attached to remains an Act of Allah Almighty.

We know that love is one of the pivotal aspects of marriage therefore it is vital that we have a true and wholesome understanding of what it means within the context of marital life.

So many individuals understand love to be that which is felt in the initial lustful stages of marriage; those moments of frequent intimacy and the times when everything was agreeably peaceful. Unfortunately, that is not what is involved in love; love is far deeper and consists of much more in the way of substance.

Love is understood differently by the sexes. How a man feels love, differs from how a woman feels love. This in itself is something that many fail to fully appreciate thereby leading to disconnection between spouses within marriage.

In order to fully appreciate this topic, I feel it is important to discuss love in the two different contexts that we may know it.

Firstly, I wish to discuss the "love" that we have all been exposed to through Hollywood and Bollywood. This perception of heightened emotion overcoming two individuals who are instantly drawn towards one another; where fate brings them together, and no force can keep them apart. This is the nicely packaged version of love; an emotion that defies all obstacles and struggles and it unites two hearts unconditionally. However, this packaging of love, in my opinion, is rather shallow and myopic; essentially, it only addresses the lust that exists between two individuals who become blinded by their desires, wishing to taste the fulfilment of their base needs.

This, my dear brothers and sisters, is not love. This is simply a reflection and crude celebration of our most humanistic trait; our craving for intimate companionship. This can be fulfilled between any man and any woman, out with the sanctimony of marriage – sadly, a rising trend. Nevertheless, we see from such immorality, there remains a general emptiness that these individuals carry within themselves. What they failed to understand was that love is not simply the enjoyment one gains from sex, love is deeper and more profound; it is an emotion based upon a multitude of understandings between two hearts that speak to one another, even in silence.

This brings me onto the second context of love, and that is one that relates to our understanding of it through an Islamic perspective. The highest form of love that any of us can ever attain is the love for Allah Subhanhu wa ta'Ala. It is a love that is increased when we increase in our actions of obedience towards Him. We can understand how love can be understood even within a Muslim marriage when we relate to our love for Allah. We seek to fulfil the rights of our spouse knowing that it is a command from Allah, and by doing so, we in turn, secure the love of Allah. This focus in our love creates a beautiful cycle that is rooted to our understanding that every action and every fulfilment of our spouse's right is a means of gaining reward from Allah, and so we do not then attach our expectations to immediate gratification from our partner, and instead find ourselves consumed in the peace that this form of worship brings.

That, my dear brothers and sisters, is the theory behind this concept, but as promised, I do not intend to just offer the theoretical ideals; I wish to place these into the realm of our realities so that we can understand them completely.

This therefore begs the question; what is love, in reality? When we truly grasp the answer to this question, we start to understand that love is foundational to every marriage.

As I touched upon earlier, love is reflected differently depending on the vessel carrying it – each individual views this emotion differently. More broadly, we can appreciate the differences between the genders.

Men understand love through respect and obedience; when a woman is careful in honouring her husband's reputation, his property and his dignity, he instantly feels a sense of security and adoration towards that woman. This feeling is heightened further when a man's every opinion and request is not challenged. Men naturally seek to provide protection for their home, for them to feel that every suggestion they put forward for the benefit of their family is disregarded or dismissed; they interpret this as being an indirect questioning of their ability to fulfil this role. That is not to say that in order for a man to feel loved a woman should simply submit to everything that her husband requests; a respectful and loving relationship will always involve a husband who also understands the beauty of seeking counsel from his wife where appropriate, and then reaching decisions which are mutually accepted. However, it is vital for women to know that this basic principle is key to securing the trust with one's husband, hence the challenging nature of marriage.

With regards to women, their understanding of love is very different. Women are highly communicative and emotional creatures; they understand love through more subtle means. When a man recognises the small details in his wife's actions or speech, this instantly ignites a sense of love within a woman. In the most simplistic terms, women equate love to appreciation. If you appreciate the seemingly small things that she does for you consistently, every day, you will instantly see a change in her perception of how much she feels loved by you. In addition, they also understand appreciation through the degree of attentiveness shown to them; there is nothing that makes a woman feel more undervalued than a husband who barely listens to her when she has waited all day to be reunited with him.

The language of love is clearly very different, and when these differences are unknown to both parties, then this leads to disengagement, regardless of both husband and wife emotionally loving one another.

To depict this more clearly, let me use the example that I touched upon earlier. At the end of a long day, a husband and wife have spent their whole day apart, both busy within their own work; as this day draws to an end, each comes home to their spouse. From the majority female perspective, there is a desire to converse about how her day has been, whereas most men will want to come home and simply shut down for a period of time, in order to recharge, and then offer more valuable family time. If this is the behavioural difference between a husband and wife then there is the potential for issues arising if this is left uncommunicated. A wife may start to feel unloved and uncared for because her husband seems distant and inattentive, whereas the husband may feel overwhelmed and agitated because his wife does not appreciate his need for down-time. Though both are expressing love through the intentions in their actions, each party is unable to understand the expression as they have failed to stop and really listen to the needs of their spouse.

Another such example relates to the ways in which men and women seek acknowledgement of their spouses' love for them. Naturally, we all find ourselves testing the extent of the love that other's harbour for us and this is something that most certainly exists in marriage. From personal experience, I have seen women assess their husband's love for them by seeking their attention; with the husband's responsiveness in obliging with his attention being an indicator for his supposed love. A prime example would be when a wife shares details of an event that are important to her, at such times, she seeks the undivided attention of her husband; if he seems distracted or dismissive of the conversation, this automatically leaves the wife feeling unimportant, which is often equated to being under-loved.

Similarly, men will gauge their wife's love for them by assessing their tolerance and sincerity towards them. The majority of men do not like to be too dependent on anyone, and so when they ask their wives to assist them in any way, this usually takes a degree of "courage". If a man's request is met with instant disdain or, worse still, it is refused, this leaves a man feeling rejected. His understanding of love is to be respected and accepted so when he humbles himself to ask his wife of any request, he hopes that she will reciprocate the humility, and recognise his desire for her to willingly please him by obliging.

Throughout marriage, love is being sought by both parties and ideally, it is being shown by both parties. What is vital to highlight here is that all too often, we become too focused on our personal needs, and less so on our partner's needs. This is not the purpose of marriage. There is no point in love if one only wishes to own it for themselves; love is at its most beautiful when it is embraced and shared so selflessly, in the hope that by spreading it, much more of it returns to us.

In essence, the more that we exude love in our marriage, the more we will feel love. As a husband, I advise you to be aware of your wife's needs; the more that you feed her need for appreciation and attention, the more you will feel her becoming supple and soft towards your needs. She spends her days tirelessly looking to do her best by you, and often you will be unaware of her every efforts, but honour her by being present with her when you finally do spend time together.

Similarly, wives, in order for you to attain and retain the love of your husband, focus on his needs; be aware of the fact that he is well aware that you are only human, and he knows that you will not simply bow to everything he asks of you, but he is very aware of your desire to keep him happy, and it is this factor that is so pivotal in his eyes. If a husband sees no sincerity in the "care" that is shown to him, naturally these actions start to feel empty – in other words, it is the concern and the regard that is shown towards him that makes him feel cared for.

With these principles understood, it is vital that we also understand how love adapts within a marriage, and how love is demonstrated in a multitude of ways.

As a marriage progresses, the nature of love should also, ideally, change with it. How we love our spouses in the early years is very different to how we love our spouses in later years; though the same basic ingredients should always exist.

In the early years of marriage, love is demonstrated through various "exciting" methods. A husband may be inclined to gift his wife with various things on a regular basis, demonstrating his devotion towards his wife. Similarly, a wife may be inclined towards cooking her husband every meal that he desires, and is always made up beautifully when receiving him upon his arrival home each evening. Such small but regular acts of love are easy in the early part of one's married life – simply due to the fact that both parties are meeting one another with excitement and reciprocation of such feelings. However, as time passes, and life's monotony and stresses seep in, such actions generally become less frequent, and there is often a danger of marital life becoming dull and stale.

With this natural and completely normal shift in married life, it is vital that we appreciate that the love is still there, but has just changed in its appearance.

For example, your wife allowing you to sleep in on a Sunday whilst she gets some housework done, is her way of showing that she loves you, and she wants you to be able to enjoy a well-deserved rest, and by setting her daily tasks aside before you wake, she then has more time to devote to you for the remainder of that day. Similarly, something as small as your husband offering to pick up a takeaway on the way home is his way of showing that he wants you to have a night off cooking so that you can both just relax together without worrying about dinner and dishes.

A beautiful example from our Prophet (saw) can be appreciated in the following hadith:

A'isha (RadyaAllahu anha) reported that the Prophet (sallallahu alayhi wasallam) would give her a vessel to drink, when she was menstruating, then he would look for the spot where she had put her lips on, and would put his lips on the same spot.
[An-Nasai & Al-Albani]

It seems so trivial but the gravity of such a small act can have huge impacts on the heart of our spouse. Our Prophet (saw) was always teaching us through his own actions how easy it can be to secure affection in a relationship.

There are many ways that longstanding married people say they love one another without actually uttering the words. I know many men who defrost their wife's car before they set off to work in the morning, knowing that they don't want her to be burdened with the hassle of it, and some men who ensure that the rubbish is taken out in order to save their wife the hardship.

Similarly, any wife who has had to leave her husband for the day, or even for a number of days, will generally leave him some meals cooked and enough clothes washed and ironed, in order to ensure that he is well-cared for. These little things often get lost in the monotony of daily routine but each action speaks loudly of the love that exists between two individuals; each action is a confession of commitment to that person, yet too often, it falls on deaf ears.

This brings me back to my earlier point, when we are too absorbed in our own needs we become blind to the daily show of love that our spouse is demonstrating to us. When this becomes the norm within a marriage it leads to two individuals who no longer value one another, and in due course, this leads to a disintegration of what was actually a healthy and normal marital situation.

In all my years of assisting married couples, the most common complaint regarding love that is aired by men is that they feel that their wife's regular arguing with them on decisions, made them feel unloved, whereas for women, it was their husband's lack of acknowledgement of the compromises they continually make. So how does one ensure that these situations are addressed before they become toxic to the relationship?

Primarily, we need to understand that men and women perceive love differently, and so we have to be careful that we do not allow our own ego to go on and bruise the ego of our spouse. For example, it may be that a wife feels that her husband does not recognise her regular compromises for him and so in order to make a stand about that, rather than communicating the issue at the root matter, she opts to intentionally disagree with her husband, in order to validate her position. This creates a vicious cycle that causes the undervaluing of spouses to escalate. By no means am I saying that one party is at greater fault than another, as marriage is about the balance between two individuals. I am merely highlighting that it takes one person to step back and say "enough" for the sake of ensuring healthy discourse. This in itself takes a lot of love and compassion, and that is why Allah describes marriage as being a union within which these two factors are so vital.

It is through our love and mercy for our spouse that we find ourselves backing down and forgiving their shortcomings – so when love and mercy begin to dissipate, we find spouses becoming less forgiving and more intolerant of one another.

Similarly, when a husband feels that his wife does not meet him with the sincerity and love, he may withdraw and become distant, leading to his wife feeling even more undervalued and so creating this ever-increasing distance between them.

In both situations, communication is vital. If one continues to assume that their partner does not love them due to how we perceive their actions, this creates multiple smokescreens within our own minds leading to a stagnant and broken relationship.

Furthermore, building upon a point I touched on earlier, when we understand that marriage is a means by which we are furthering our worship of Allah, and we keep this point at the forefront of our minds throughout our married lives, we start to really increase on our desire to be tolerant. When we are constantly remembering our duty and accountability before Allah, we take greater care in ensuring that we are not abusing the trust that our spouse is owed. In addition, we are less willing to hold onto the shortfalls of our spouses, and are more inclined towards forgiveness.

The Prophet sallallahu alayhi wasallam said:
"Allah is only Merciful with those who show mercy to others."
[Sahih Bukhari]

When we look at the Prophetic examples of love, we are reminded of the softness that a man needs to show his wife and the tolerance that he shows when her emotions naturally err. Furthermore, when we look at the Mothers of the Believers, we see examples of women who sacrificed much in order to *support* their husband. Many argue that these examples are rather fantastical in their nature as modern-day men are not of the calibre of the Prophet (saw) and modern-day women cannot be equated to the Mother of the Believers. Just that statement is a reflection of why we are on such dire straits; none of us will ever reach the heights of the most pious of creation, but they have been sent as examples for us so that we may at least *strive* towards the goodness that they taught. Such a defeatist attitude has no place in the psyche of any Muslim, let alone in the mind-set of two Muslims who have promised to be one another's companions on the road to Jannah. As husband and wife, neither should ever shy away from inviting their spouse back onto the path towards goodness – that is the most pure example of their love for you – their desire to be eternally in your companionship, in'shaa'Allah.

In conclusion, it is truly foolish to believe that love is the sole ingredient for the survival of marriage. Love is one of many ingredients that are essential for marriage to be made easier and happier

– but by no means can a marriage survive purely on the existence of love alone, especially when love is easily misunderstood as the journey of marriage unfolds.

Life Lesson 2:

"Do not be fooled by what other's told you of love. Look and listen carefully for how love appears and speaks to you in life, it can be seen and found in the most mundane of daily moments; do not look passed it."

CHAPTER 6

Myth no. 3 – My Spouse Completes Me

Anas (radyAllahu anhu) reported that the Prophet (sallallahu alayhi wasallam) said:
"Whomever Allah blesses with a righteous wife, He has helped him with half of his religion, so let him fear Allah with regard to the other half."
[Al-Haakim]

When we get married there are many expectations that we seem to develop prior to consolidating our life with another person. Seemingly, the most dangerous of these is the assumption that one's spouse is the completion of one's own self.

When we read the above hadith, it may seem correct to assume that our marriage is the completion of our lives; a good marriage certainly does serve to do this, but we must not misunderstand the statement. When we marry, half of our Deen is "taken care of", but we are thereby advised to ensure that we take great care of the other half of it; the half that lies within our own hands.

Ma'shaa'Allah our beautiful Deen is one that encourages proactivity; it is not a faith of complacency. We are encouraged to work hard with our own hands and reap the fruits of our efforts - and this concept applies to marriage as well.

If we allow the Hollywood narrative, so romantically declared by Tom Cruise in *Jerry Maguire*, about how his romantic interest was the completion of him, we allow ourselves to fall into a misconception about how our spouse serves us.

Each of us would have heard the positive psychology statements that we are exposed to regarding happiness being something that we need to attain from within ourselves and not sought through others; this exact concept needs to be understood in marriage.

Marriage is one of the most selfless and compromising promises that one makes in life; marriage is a statement of "I have given myself to you, unconditionally, and I will seek to make you happy in every way that I can". This is a statement that needs to be equally met and understood by both parties, or else there is an unhappy imbalance that creeps into the unity.

If you walk into marriage expecting your spouse to dispel your personal unhappiness, know that you have set yourself up for disappointment. Marriage requires you to be healthy and content as an individual, so that you can be an emotional and physical support for your spouse. If you have no aspiration to seek your own internal happiness, know that you will not find it through other means. Happiness is something that needs to exist within ourselves. We need to be happy with our own physical appearance and not await the appraisal of others before we believe in our own beauty. We need to believe that we are valuable and worthy, and not seek that accolade from the behaviours of others towards us. We need to possess confidence and assertiveness and not expect this to be something that we attain from the approval of those around us.

The moment we cultivate a healthy mind set about ourselves; that is when we have freed ourselves from the misery that comes from seeking acceptance in places we may never attain it.

I know a particular couple who married one another without fully understanding the hidden expectations each party held about the other. The husband had experienced a life of low self-esteem, and was elated when his wife agreed to marrying him, as he had fallen into such a state of self-deprecation, he never thought himself able to secure the love of such an attractive woman. The wife, she too had experienced many difficulties in life, she was hoping to escape the unhappiness within her own mind through the love that she sought in marriage.

Here we see two emotionally and mentally weak individuals, both coming together in the name of love, hoping that marriage would appease their internal struggles. In reality, what came to be was that with time, the husband became very possessive and controlling of his wife, as he was afraid that he would lose her to another man, and the wife became increasingly frustrated because all she yearned for was the security and affection of her husband.

Though they remain married, they are far from happy in their situation; the two struggle together for the sake of the children they have, but neither has attained the expectation they entered into marriage with.

This case alone shows how vital it is for us to ensure that we have a sound understanding of who we are before we even consider embarking upon the path of marriage; if you do not know your own weaknesses, or your own strengths, how can you expect to coexist with someone in a healthy manner?

For those of us who are already married, and see this factoring into our own marriage, it is not too late to change the mould. Speaking with your spouse about things openly and transparently helps to air any misconceptions that have begun to grow throughout your marriage, and it offers opportunity to discuss means by which to improve situations.

Naturally, we all carry emotional baggage throughout life, but it is important that we do not view our spouse as a means of simply off-loading that burden. Alhamdulillah, the blessed nature of a healthy marriage is the desire to support and assist your partner, but as Muslims, it is also vital that we are able to self-sustain a healthy psyche.

A really healthy habit for maintaining a clear mind is through journaling. This is a highly underrated act. SubhanAllah, this was something similar to what our blessed Prophet sallallahu alayhi wasallam did when he would isolate himself in the Cave in Mount Hirra; it would be a means for soul-searching, and self-evaluation.

There is no greater time in one's life where this act is more necessary than when married; timeout is something that is essential in order to organise thoughts and emotions, and it allows us to effectively prioritise those things that require communication, and those things that are simply "momentary emotional outbursts".

For those of you not already doing this, I would strongly advise that you embrace this habit, and I assure you, your mind will feel freer and healthier, and more present in the moments that matter in your life.

There is no denying that there is a very romantic analogy created in that statement *"You complete me"*, but in truth, marriage is about complimenting your spouse beautifully; it is about understanding and accepting the flaws of your spouse, and knowing that with you by their side, those flaws become less apparent – so you are not a completion of another person, but a means by which their true beauty is enhanced, and a means by which their weaknesses and flaws are masked through understanding their strengths.

There is no truer and more beautiful analogy of this concept than the words of our Lord:

"...They are your garments, and you are their garments."
[Al Baqarah, 2: part verse 187]

What is a garment?
When we are clothed, our physical imperfections are concealed; our most vulnerable state is hidden. Similarly, our spouse is the one person that knows our vulnerabilities and our imperfections, and seeks to cover these with their own selves.

Our clothes keep us warm, and they act as a means of protection from the elements around us – in that same way, it is our spouse who ultimately serves to protect us. They would rather harm touch them, than allowing it to find their spouse.

Our clothing sits over our bodies, in direct contact with our skin. It is our clothing that wraps around us so closely, and in that way too, our spouse is the only one that Allah has ordained as being our intimate companion, the one whose own body, envelopes our own,

42

when husband and wife engage in intercourse.

Our clothing is a means of comfort as well, undoubtedly, each of us has a favourite item of clothing that when worn, instantly allows us to feel easy and comfortable. So too, is your spouse; the source of comfort and ease at times of distress.

Each of these aspects highlights the fact that your "garment" is not something that *makes* you, but in reality, your "garment" enhances your existing beauty, and allows you to be at ease within yourself.

This brings me back to my earlier point. Marriage needs both parties to be ready to serve that purpose *for* their spouse; however, if *our expectations* of our spouse are all that we have focused upon, then this will inevitably lead to unease as the marriage progresses. The more that we focus on how we are hoping to be that garment, the more we will find that Allah will open the way for our spouse to reciprocate that same desire to serve our own needs.

Alhamdulillah, it is clear to see that we do not have to look to any other narrative beyond that of our Qur'an and Sunnah in order for us to see the beauty in which a husband and wife are compliments of one another; one does not need the other to complete them, our completion comes through our servitude to Allah – but our spouses, Alhamdulillah, they are our companions in reaching that closeness to Allah, and in'shaa'Allah, when chosen wisely, a means by which that path is made easier.

Life Lesson 3:

"Do not hope that another soul will be able to fix your broken state. Seek to attain a healthy mind, a place where you are happy to exist, only then are you ready to share your exceptional beauty, without any need or expectation."

CHAPTER 7:

Myth no. 4 – Love is Reason Enough to Change

It is the instinctive nature of love that blinds us into believing that perfection exists within a person; this very element of love lies at the root of many marital problems.

Prior to marriage, we all seem to have a notion that the person we are looking to marry is either perfect and without any flaws, or their flaws are easily overlooked and will be of no impact. It is only with time that we realise that both of these aspects are completely mythical – both concepts are quite literally shattered when we venture into the realities of marriage.

In the early courting stages, our hormones and heightened desire often prevent us from seeking out the deeper matters that we will inevitably need for a healthy marital life. In particular, many women face societal pressures to be married within a certain time frame, and so will allow themselves to compromise on the most fundamental characteristics in their prospective spouse.

I cannot stress enough the importance of knowing your own self prior to considering marriage; you need to understand your own strengths, hopes, aspirations and weaknesses, in order to understand what characteristics you wish to secure in a spouse. Many fail to do this simple yet vital exercise, and find themselves seeking to change the person they marry. Unfortunately, the system does not work like that.

From personal observation, I have seen many marriages fall into this very trap, and it can be an incredibly detrimental issue if mismanaged.

A particular couple that comes to mind began their courting in their late teens, without familial involvement. Their relationship progressed heavily based upon physical attraction, and both parties were aware of the other's shortcomings however, their desire to marry forced them to set these matters aside; unexplored and barely discussed.

With them then married, their first year of marriage threw them into turmoil, realising that their compatibility was almost non-existent.

The husband had hoped to mould his wife into a more practicing Muslim woman and desired that she developed a softer personality towards him – in reality, his wife's nature and personality had been long-established as being coarse and demeaning, leaving his expectations unfounded, and quite simply, unrealistic.

The wife had become accustomed to her personal understanding of what she believed her husband's personality to be; open, flexible, and completely accepting of her ways – in reality, her husband had adopted this approach believing that this was the best tact in securing her as a wife. Their marriage became a battle of enforcing change upon one another; a husband disillusioned by his wife's temperament and a wife enraged by her husband's false personality.

It is clear to see that in marriage, there are certain matters that need to be explored completely and maturely, setting aside the desire to explore one's sexual urges. Do not let satan overcome you with seeking base fulfilment but remind yourself of the Prophetic teachings and the fundamental characteristics that we should seek in our spouses:

The Prophet sallallahu alayhi wasallam said:
"If someone with whose piety and character you are satisfied with comes to you, marry (to) him. If you do not do so, there will be trials in the earth and a great deal of evil."
[at-Tirmidhi]
Abdullah ibn Amr reported: The Prophet sallallahu alayhi

wasallam said'
"The world is provision, and the best provision in the world
is a righteous woman."
[Sahih Muslim]

The above two hadith quite clearly highlight the most important characteristic that we should look for; piety.

When piety exists deeply within an individual, you will also find that that person will naturally be tolerant; they will naturally aspire to commit actions that will be pleasing to Allah, and by default seek to ensure their spouse's happiness.

Do not misunderstand me, even amongst the most pious, marriage remains a struggle, but it is a struggle that always seeks to bring the focus back to pleasing Allah. Furthermore, piety is only something that is truly appreciated by one who possesses this within themselves:

"...Good women are for good men, and good men are for
good women..."
[Surah an-Nur, 24: part verse 26]

This verse indicates that we aspire to be the best in order to attain the best and it also highlights the importance of compatibility.

From the outset this concept should be ingrained within our psyche; do not seek to marry simply to fulfil a Sunnah, but first seek to understand what the demands and rights of this Sunnah are, and then establish how able you are in fulfilling these pillars. I have mentioned earlier, and will emphasise yet again, marriage starts with your own self; your primary focus should be what you have to have offer another person. Too many problems arise because of such heavy oversight of this key quality.

Once this has been established, it is then that we are in a position of strength to seek a partner that is truest to our nature. Do not fall into the common trap of establishing a superficial sense of commitment only to find that the person of choice holds no depth in your heart; the physical beauties wear away with time, but these deeper emotional connections only grow in strength.

I would strongly advise for those not yet married, devise a checklist of elements that you feel you cannot compromise upon, and when pursuing a potential suitor, ensure that this is used as a reference point prior to committing to marriage.

Understandably, for those who are married, this is an issue that requires completely different management. If you have married someone whom you thought would change with time, then unfortunately, it needs to be understood that this cannot be a point of reliance in maintaining the health of a marriage.

To expect people to change significantly is a big ask; naturally, when entering into marriage, each party assumes that they will be loved and adored for simply being who they are. After all, the notion of love is to accept the flaws of your beloved knowing that their nuances are endearing as they form part of the beauty of their entirety.

When married, we find ourselves pushed to our limits by our spouses "flaws", it is then vital we contextualise that flaw whilst also establishing how best to deal with it.

Firstly, we must always remember that satan has made it his objective to cause rifts between couples. It is one of his many tricks to have couples argue over minor things that have become magnified in their minds. So when finding yourself irritated by your spouse, seek refuge in Allah from the plots of satan:

"My Lord, I seek refuge in You from the incitements of the devils,
And I seek refuge in You, My Lord, lest they be present with me."
[Surah al-Mu'minum, 23: verses 97-98]

Secondly, do not deal with the matter whilst in a state of irritation; this will achieve no results, it will simply cause the situation to escalate beyond necessary bounds. Take your time and journal your thoughts – why has this issue started to cause you annoyance now, and what is it about your spouse's habit that specifically causes you upset? When we force ourselves to analyse in a more logical and clinical manner, we are able to see beyond what may simply be a hyper-emotional response.

Thirdly, ask yourself whether your spouse's habit is one that cannot be outweighed by their many good characteristics. A personal hint for each of you is to have a list of five points that you adore about your partner; have them saved on your smartphone, or keep them close to hand – make a point of pondering over this list regularly – remind yourself of why you love one another, as it is satan who wants you to forget.

Let us never forget that we possess a multitude of flaws, and these are things that our spouse's tolerate of us. Patience is the key to success in this element of marriage, and a proactive desire in reminding ourselves of the good that we see from our spouse's daily.

Do not become a person who ransoms their spouse to changing or else being abandoned by you; that is no way to attaining the desired goal. Open the doors to communication and discuss concerns with softness and mercy, having the intention to achieve peace between one another at the forefront of your mind.

With that said, there will be some cases in which the glaring incompatibility that exists between two individuals is just too much to endure. Again, maturity and communication is key to discussing the best path forwards.

"Must every house be built on love? What about loyalty and appreciation?"
[Umar bin Khattab, radyAllahu anhu]

Love is undoubtedly a beautiful union between two individuals, but love requires us to accept our beloved as they are. Love does not demand for the change of a person, so they are completely altered from their true self. Indeed, there is no harm in journeying through marriage and assisting each other towards goodness in every aspect of life, but forcing someone to be that which they are not ready to become; this becomes an injustice and a source of animosity in a place where there should be love and tolerance.

Life Lesson 4:

"Each of us is a beautifully perfect tapestry, woven from our own unique flaws; to deny the flaws, is to deny the beauty that we claim to love in that individual."

CHAPTER 8:

Myth no. 5 – Talking Comes Easy

As marriage first begins, newlyweds are almost inseparable. If not physically together, then mentally, they remain in each other's thoughts, with frequent calls and messages passing between them. This is the beauty of the early stages of marriage; there is a longing that exists with every separation.

As much as every married couple would love for this to be the life-long reality, sadly it is not the way. Similar to the honeymoon bliss, a lot of couples fall into the delusion that they will hold onto this soft and gentle approach that comes easy in the early stages of marriage. Argumentation is avoided during the first stages of marriage because both parties are very willing to compromise and please the other. Naturally, with time, this becomes an unsustainable scenario. Couples begin to feel the pressure of constantly submitting and finding themselves in situations where they have to accept circumstances that may be far from pleasing for them.

So, what to do?

Firstly, one must be clever enough to understand that every relationship has its ups and its downs. That's completely natural and completely healthy. You have spent a lifetime with parents and/or siblings – did you not have the occasional exchange of strong words with them? Did such exchanges lead to the end of your relationship?

The marital relationship, in this aspect is more intense than in any other relationship. When we live in such close proximity with another person, constantly in one another's pockets, abrasion between each party is highly likely, especially when intertwined with daily stresses. We must be confident in our relationship and know that we possess the maturity and intelligence to manage our communication cleverly. As is often the case in marital discord, it is the little things that go unaddressed that build up and lead to pent up pressure in one or both parties.

We will never see the world from the exact perspective of another person, and inevitably, this will lead to some difference in opinion, and that is completely okay. Alhamdulillah, it is this very thing that makes life so beautifully diverse. If everyone was to be the same, things would quite quickly become boring.

How we communicate with anyone determines how that relationship grows; our tone will very often say more than our words.

Naturally, when we are in a relationship, we see our spouse daily, we become very relaxed and at-ease with one another. This can have two potential effects; firstly, it may be that this easy nature with one another leads to an abuse of how we deal with one another – our partner may become the one person that never sees politeness from us, and instead deals with all our negative and temperamental aspects. On the other hand, it may be that this relaxed existence with one another provides the basis for the communications between husband and wife being optimal; they become that one person that you simply look at, and they know what you are thinking, they become that one person that you know you can drop your inhibitions with, and just be that little bit crazy, and still be loved.

We hold the key as to how this degree of relaxed existence will impact our relationship – it is within our hands to decide whether we use this to build our relationship, or potentially destroy it.

How many of us can relate to a scenario when we said something to our partner, and their reaction was completely disproportionate to what we meant? All too often, we simply say things to one another, but do not actually stop to think how our words may be perceived.

It is very easy to just say what is on our mind, but we must take great care with this; our partner is a trust upon us from Allah, how we treat them through words, actions and affections, will be questioned by Allah on our Last Day. Any hurt, whether intended or not, will be something that we are answerable for.

Throughout this book, you will have noted my reference to timing of communication and the tone. These are invaluable things to store in our minds, and apply immediately to our marriage, and other relationships.

TIMING:

Within a marriage it is vital that we make it our business to be aware of our spouse's behavioural and mood patterns. We all have our off-moments, and we all have our personal anxieties that we carry in our minds. The more sensitive we become to these aspects of our spouse, the more attuned we will become to timing any critical communication well.

We should also take a moment and ask ourselves how we would like to hear criticism from our spouse; would we want to be "slapped down" with harsh words or blunt criticism, or would we rather that criticism is delivered with care and consideration? It may seem difficult to apply in reality, but all it takes of us is to pause a moment, and ask ourselves whether the conditions seem right to speak out.

For example, a spouse coming in from work, most likely is tired, so any heavy conversation is not going to be well received. At these times of day, it is best to keep the conversation light and easy. Where there is a need to discuss important matters, it is actually wise to ask your spouse to allocate time, so both of you are in the correct frame of mind to have an in-depth discussion, whilst also ensuring that you are not open to distractions.

TONE:

How we articulate our words inevitably has a massive bearing upon how they are received. Poorly used tone can have a huge impact on a relationship. For example, where there is a partner who is consistently condescending in their manner and tone, they will automatically rob their spouse of any confidence. It is the duty of each of us as a spouse to support our partner, even when criticising. Naseehah is the Arabic for offering advice/criticism, when wishing to see a good result for our brother or sister. This is something that constantly passes between a husband and wife. We should constantly be offering each other supportive words in order to see one another flourish into the best versions of ourselves.

Though most married couples will claim that they only ever offer their spouse words of advice, intended with goodness, there is a common failure in appreciating the tone in which those words are delivered, and it is here that even the best naseehah fails to touch the heart.

KNOW YOUR LIMITS:

Granted, there will be moments throughout marriage when even our best attempts in communications appear to fail; this is when we must embrace the concept of a *sincere apology*.

There is nothing more encouraging and more healing in a relationship than an apology that is said from the heart, in the hope that it is felt by the heart of the recipient. In saying this, there is a process that we must go through in our own minds to ensure that our apology is well received.

Firstly, know what it is you are apologising for; there is nothing more soul-destroying than an empty *sorry*; when someone sees that they have exceeded your limits, and simply throws out a sorry in the hope that it will make things instantly better. It is your duty as a spouse to seek to understand why your spouse was hurt by your words or actions. By endeavouring upon that path of understanding, you show your partner that you care, and that you value your relationship, and you are eager to learn from error, and in'shaa'Allah, protect one another from repeating that same cycle of hurt.

Secondly, do not use an apology to justify your actions. An apology should simply be a means of creating closure. There will be better opportunities in which you and your spouse can discuss why certain things happen, but this must not happen at a time when you are trying to make peace between one another.

Lastly, show that you are sorry. Once you have understood the reason for apologising, and effectively delivered the apology, you must demonstrate this apology by doing your utmost to ensure that it is something that you will aim to avoid in future. We all know the pain that comes from being hurt by the same person, in the same way, again, and again. It is a cycle that we, as individuals, must take ownership for in our own relationships.

KEEPING THE PEACE:

There is no greater hope from marriage than an existence in peace with your companion. There is no better way in attaining this than through learning to communicate effectively and wisely.

In marriage, as mentioned earlier, your spouse is like your garment; the nearest thing to your own skin, your protector and your comfort. Your spouse should provide you the security that you seek at your most vulnerable, and this security is gained through the bridge of communication.

At our lowest points, we should not feel ashamed or afraid to feel how we feel, and as husband or wife, it is our duty to ensure that we do not dishonour our spouse by dismissing how they feel. In marriage, there should be no guilt, or shame in sharing our inner thoughts and worries, there should be no fear of judgement or feeling that our every emotion needs justification. As a spouse, we owe our partner the security in their own natural vulnerability, as each of us has our own weaknesses and these weaknesses, once manifest, should be protected by our spouse rather than being further exposed.

A common problem that couples have complained to me about in this matter emphasises the difference in communication between men and women.

Women are highly communicative in nature, they gauge a strong connection based upon how well communication is reciprocated, and they are eager to discuss the depths of feelings through regular and in-depth conversation. Men on the other hand, are less inclined to explore emotions in-depth, they are more logical in their approach and can, at times, find too much emotion to be somewhat burdensome.

Furthermore, when couples engage in an emotion-based dialogue, women generally seek to simply vocalise their concerns to attentive ears, whereas by nature, men feel they need to provide a solution to any problems presented. This misunderstanding of what is needed can often create distance between husband and wife simply because the husband feels unable to provide a solution, whilst the wife in actual fact, only wants her husband's attention and physical comfort.

I am certain that every man reading this book will be able to relate to those times when their wife just breaks down into tears, and you have no idea why, or how, or what caused the emotional flurry. Instinctively, most men freeze in such circumstances, not because they do not care but because they care so much; their inability to help their wives in their state of sadness causes them to feel agitated with themselves as they have no way of fixing the situation. So here is the good news; husbands, you do not have to fix this, all you need to do is walk up to your wife, embrace her tightly, and allow her to cry into you – she knows that you are there for her physically and emotionally, supporting her, and not dismissing her needs. Alhamdulillah that is all it takes to bring some solidity back into your relationship.

There will be times when we do not understand one another, and we fail to comprehend our partner's behaviour or actions; let the dust settle, but do not let these matters go unchecked. It is vital that we discuss events in our marriage that impact us and we gain explanations or seek to understand why things played out a certain way. If we do not follow through with our spouse, the wall of silence will slowly build between you.

This is where empathy is so important in a relationship, and it is something that can only truly flourish when there is uninhibited communication between husband and wife. Empathy rids a relationship of selfishness and it forces a relationship to become more about understanding and fulfilling the needs of our partner.

MYTH NO. 5

It is a myth that communication is easy in marriage; it begins easy, but as with all aspects of marriage, with time, in order for it to be sustained, conscious effort needs to be applied; communication is no different. If husbands and wives do not make time to work on this key pillar of their relationship, then inevitably their marriage becomes a hollow co-existence of two strangers who once knew one another.

Life Lesson 5:

"We must not speak, simply to be heard, we must speak with purpose and intention. When we hope to articulate from the love that exists in our hearts, with the hope to mend the situation before us, it is only then that our words can touch the hearts of our beloved."

CHAPTER 9:

Myth no. 6 – Then Comes Baby to Make Things Even Better

The purpose of marriage is to establish love and mercy between two people, and for them to then go on and procreate, and bring up good, God-fearing children, so they may serve as an ongoing legacy in the service of Allah.

Naturally, every couple seeks to share the journey of parenthood together as a means of strengthening their own relationship, whilst also expanding the bounty within their home through the blessings that are attached with offspring.

However, too many couples fail to comprehend the stress and strain that comes with the role of parenthood, and how this job completely modifies the dynamic of a relationship.

Through discussions with couples who have young children, I have come to see a sad pattern emerging in marriage. Again, this is a rather generalised observation, but one that I have seen to be on the rise. Most couples will end up having children within the first two years of their marriage after having enjoyed a healthy honeymoon period, and then agreeing to try to conceive. When a woman falls pregnant, her body undergoes a multitude of changes and strains, and the effects of these can last beyond the 9 month period of pregnancy; during these months, the intimacy that may once have been regular and fulfilling, almost completely falls away, and most husbands understand this, though more than likely, suffer due to it. Due to the extent of strain that a woman feels throughout this period, she may feel annoyed at the mere inclination of her husband's desires, which in the long-term can create distance between the two parties. Once a child is brought into this weakened situation, what tends to happen is that the lack of contact between husband and wife broadens. The couple now no longer behaves as a couple, instead their lives become centred round their child's need, and their own needs are neglected.

A lot of men have spoken to me personally about their feeling of isolation and neglect when their relationship moved to parenthood; they found that their wives had no time for them because they were so consumed with caring for their young child. Similarly, women complained that once parenting became a part of their marriage, their husbands were less available to them and less present when they needed their support.

What we fail to realise when we find ourselves in this situation is that we assume that parenting is a role that we do on our own. Mothers seem to feel that the child is primarily their responsibility, and fathers feel lost in how best to assist the situation.

Children are supposed to make a happier marriage, but all too often, their addition into marriage causes an unexpected collapse between couples.

This does not have to be the way.

Parenting is something that needs to happen together, it needs to be something that both parties take full responsibility for. Fathers should not feel like they should be championed for having changed their child's nappy when their wife does so over a dozen times in a day. Similarly women should not martyr themselves in caring for their children, whilst failing to allocate time that their husband needs. The more that the burden of care is shared between husband and wife, the stronger the relationship becomes, whilst setting a solid example to your children on how a healthy relationship should be.

This concept can be used as a means of flirting with one another, for example, a husband can rather lovingly tell his wife that he will get the kids to bed whilst she pampers herself so they can enjoy some personal time together; this is a beautiful way of demonstrating that you love your wife and want to ease her burden, and also value your relationship, and continue to invest the time that you need together in order to maintain a healthy marital status.

As your children grow up, it is vital to set precedence at an early age regarding mum and dad's private space. Children should never feel able to walk freely in and out of your bedroom, nor should they be invited into your bed unless there is dire need. When a child is poorly, or seeks parental comfort at night, one parent should sleep with them in the child's own room. This protects the sanctimony of your bedroom, and it allows you to have privacy even if it is just to have an adult conversation, and feel reconnected with one another.

In addition, whilst your children are young know that you can have your subtle adult jokes and flirtation, allowing you to maintain that chemistry with one another, without necessarily exposing your children to too much intimate contact, though there is no harm in your children seeing their parents hugging and expressing love, if anything, this is a healthy and positive environment for them to be nourished in.

There is no doubt that children are hard work, and they will bring with them a great deal of stress and struggle to a marriage, but if managed as a team that recognises that they owe each other time and devotion; children can eventually serve to bring much happiness to a marriage.

Life Lesson 6:

"The stronger you and your spouse are as a team, the easier you will face the adversity that comes with any changing dynamic within your home. Seek to solidify your companionship before you introduce new elements to your relationship."

CHAPTER 10:

Myth no. 7 – Sex isn't a Big Deal

Imaam Al Ghazali likened the act of intimacy as being a taste of paradise that we have been allowed to experience in this life. Pure and wholesome intimacy is something that is undoubtedly pleasurable beyond description, and something that distinguishes the sacred bond of marriage from any other relationship that we experience in life.

Sadly, an ever-increasing phase amongst our communities is the sheer misunderstanding of the importance of pure and halal sexual relations.

In order to fully appreciate the depths of this issue, we must analyse the current climates and mindset that our youth, and ourselves, are exposed to.

The understanding of sex has become polluted by various factors, primarily, the belittling nature with which the pornography industry, and to a lesser extent, the movie industry has created a whole new and obscene narrative to the act of intercourse.

In recent months, we have seen the much-talked about *50 Shades of Grey* being unleashed onto our cinema screens; that paired with the original novel; we have a very dangerous depiction of what a supposedly healthy sexual relationship looks like. Having not taken the time, nor the interest in reading the book or watching the film; I have heard enough about the plot and the lead characters to know that if this is what any one of our communities consumes and sees as being an accurate narrative for what they should seek in sexual intimacy, then we have a very grave situation on our hands.

50 Shades of Grey seems to suggest that it is perfectly acceptable to objectify and manipulate a female mind and body in order for a dominant male to incessantly fulfil his desire. Similarly, the pornography industry builds upon this very same notion. The gross and unapologetic objectification of females in such scenarios has poisoned the minds of many males, thinking that the act of intercourse is as it seems on the screen.

In addition, such industries rather heinously go on to depict both the male and female form in such unrealistic and unflawed manners that this, too, leads to a violation of the true appreciation of the natural and flawed beauty that each of us possesses.

Alongside this unrealistic depiction of intimacy, we also have the general marketing of products using sex as a means of capturing attention. Human nature instinctively craves the intimacy that comes from sexual experience, and this has been manipulated by marketers in order to engage the consumer. This method brings with it a serious problem; rising curiosity about sex in the minds of many single, and therefore abstinent, Muslims.

As Muslims, we do not dismiss the innate need for fulfilment of sexual desire, nor do we demean the act of intercourse as being something that is sinful when performed within marriage. However, there has been a serious failure along the way in educating and embracing the topic of sex by much of our communities, leading to the majority of individuals seeking out answers via the wrong pathways. Even in situations where our youth may not be seeking out answers, the constant exposure and bombardment to hypersexualised advertising leads to a regular ignition of the natural desires that exist in all of us, and once these desires become more prominent, instinctively, over time, fulfilment is sought. Undoubtedly, the doors to fitna become easier to open the more our weaknesses are played upon in this manner. However, Alhamdulillah, our faith celebrates sexual gratification when it is explored and fulfilled within the sacred bonds of marriage, and so we seek to secure ourselves safely into such a commitment, before satan is able to strengthen his hold on our desires.

Our social environments also play a heavy part on our understanding of sexual intimacy. SubhanAllah, increasingly in the West there is a very liberal and blasé approach to sex education. Schools are now insistent upon introducing such teachings to children as young as 5-6years old. When we really step back and think about this, we see the difficulties that arise from this. Sex is something that is being imprinted in the minds of socially immature individuals, in addition, it is being taught in a manner that does not coincide with the sanctity of our religion, and so unless we take control of this matter, we are allowing our future Muslims to be exploited by a liberalised understanding of intimacy.

Furthermore, even amongst our young adults who may have been brought up in a less sexualised climate, they are left exposed to their peers in High School, University or even in the work place, rather openly sharing personal sexual experiences, or the exposure to innuendo-laced jokes whether socially or on television. Each of these exchanges sows seeds from which further sexual curiosity grows; supposed sexual "norms" are being imposed upon us by those who hold little of the morality that we are striving to hold fast to.

With all these factors infiltrating our minds, is it any wonder that marital intimacy seems to be in disarray?

So let me wind this down a little – do not let the masses fool you; sex does matter! Sex is the distinction of marriage from all other forms of companionship, so the better we understand the concept – the more fulfilling our marriages are set to become, in'shaa'Allah.

As mentioned earlier, this topic requires a whole book in itself – however, I felt it was vital to make mention of some very important aspects of this issue, in order to assist couples in their marital journeys. For clarity, I will explore intimacy at different stages in marriage.

WEDDING NIGHT:

Once we accept the proposal of a prospective partner, the emotional drive spikes exponentially. Naturally, we become hyper aware of the nikkah opening the way to a husband and wife then going on to spending their first night together, and no doubt this brings a torrent of emotions ranging from desire-driven excitement to fearing-the-unknown-anxiety!

Before I embark upon some very important "technical" points with respect to the first night, I felt it pivotal to describe the Sunnah acts:

1. The husband recites the Prophetic dua whilst placing his right hand gently upon his wife's forehead. The dua is as follows:

Allahumma innee 'as'aluka khayrahaa wa khara majabal-tahaa 'alayhi wa 'a'oothu bika min sharrihaa wa sharri maajabaltahaa 'alayhi.
O Allah, I ask You of the goodness of her and the goodness upon which You have Created her, and I seek refuge in You from the evil of her and the evil upon which You have Created her.
[Abu Dawud 2/248]

2. The husband and wife should make wudhu and pray 2 rakah nafl together, with the husband leading his wife in prayer.

I want each of you to ponder the significance of these two acts on the Wedding Night. Each act reminds us that truly we are dependent on Allah's blessings upon as at every given moment in life – without His blessings, we cannot attain success, and in this sense, marriage is no different! This is the first step on a journey where two people have vowed to be the completion of each other's faith, what better way to begin that journey than by thanking Allah, and asking for His blessings to grace your marriage? Alhamdulillah. In addition to the blessings, these two acts allow a degree of peace to settle into the hearts of both parties, and reduce the extent of nerves felt by both.

With respect to the intimate interactions between husband and wife, I feel it is vital for both a man and a woman to appreciate their other half's mindset with respect to the wedding night, in order to ensure that the first steps upon the intimacy journey are healthy ones.

It is worth highlighting some distinctions between the male and female sexual drives; much like each gender's perception of love differing, so too does the manner and means by which each gender is aroused.

In order to depict this appropriately, let me use the analogy of a pot of water on the stove; when the gas burner is switched on, it is instantly hot – however, the pot of water takes time to heat up and come to a boil; a woman is gently aroused from the passion (heat) of her husband expressed over a period of time, whereas the man can quite instantly be aroused, much like the flame that is red hot at the touch of a button.

In the heat of the moment, it is near impossible for us to change our perspective, which is why it is vital that we know this pivotal distinction between men and women prior to endeavouring upon intimacy.

For every man, when that fog of desire begins to settle over your mind when you are first in the company of your wife; remind yourself that on this night, she desires you just as much as you desire her, but know that her longing for you equates to feeling your gentleness, she wants you to respect her fragility, and most of all she wants you to slowly gain her trust and confidence through stage-by-stage intimacy building. As a basic guideline, on that first night it is important that you start with the basics and work up; hold hands and embrace in a tender hug; start to feel comfortable with one another's body, and gently holding one another. Allow ample time for something as simple as physical contact prior to engaging in any intense intimate interaction; this will allow both parties to relax and begin to feel confident with one another. For women specifically, the more time and attention they are given the more relaxed and open to arousal they become.

There is no doubt that it is difficult for a man to restrain his advances, it is therefore important for women to understand that aspect of the male psyche; once his instinct for sexual fulfilment is ignited, he will want to show his love for you through physical intimacy, and often the urgency of his advancements equate to the height of his desire. In other words, some men may become overcome by their heightened desire on the wedding night, and this may lead to them being rather clumsy in their interaction with their wife – though, in reality, this rushed demeanour is actually an embodiment of his affection towards his spouse.

For a woman, her first experience is always going to be paired with a degree of discomfort due to penetration. In the case of unmarried, virgin women, then they will experience the breaking of the hymen tissue, and may even experience a degree of bleeding as a result of this. The apprehension that a woman understandably carries about this process, will be at the forefront of her mind on this night – she will be scared and nervous at the thought of penetration, as a result, both parties need to be assist one another in ensuring minimal discomfort.

Firstly, men, reassure your wives with love and affection that this night has been long-dreamt about by yourselves however, on this night, you want to go only as far as is comfortable for your wife. This is a very difficult sacrifice for any man to make, but it undoubtedly, is a sacrifice that will sow the seeds towards far more satisfying sex for years to come. I want to pause here for just a moment and state; men, I know the act of sexual intimacy remains a show of your love for your wife, but remember, she understands your love for her through your *appreciation* of her situation. Do not allow satan to whisper doubt into your mind about delaying consummation of marriage slightly; take advantage of enjoying the beauty of one another's bodies for the first time through general play and caressing.

Secondly, where there is unfamiliarity with the technicalities of intercourse, naturally, this leads to a lot of awkwardness. There have been many cases where men and women alike have been unable to complete penetration due to the inability to "navigate" the anatomy appropriately. Even where this is not an issue, the initial insertion can become quite tricky, leading to the act become more methodical, and less romantic! It is vital therefore, that each of us understands that the wedding night is not that Hollywood scene that has formed our daydreams for many years, it is in reality a rather awkward and messy process.

Thirdly, touching further upon the issue of discomfort with penetration, it is so deeply important that both husband and wife adequately lubricate their private parts in order to add as much comfort to intercourse as possible. Lubrication is something that we should not shy away from, and especially not in these early days of intimacy. Most women on their wedding night will have had no prior concept of arousal in that complete sense, whereas for complete arousal in men, penetration does not necessarily have to be achieved.

The more aroused a woman becomes, the more her private parts naturally become accommodating to penetration. On that first night, the likelihood of her achieving heightened arousal, amidst the apprehension, is low, so lubricating generously will provide comfort for both parties, despite the tension that may initially be felt.

To summarise, the Wedding Night is the most dreamt about moment in both of yours' lives, but we must understand that the dream of a man varies very much from that of a woman; show her that she is safe in your care and you will secure her adoration for years to come in'shaa'Allah.

HONEYMOON PHASE:

As man and wife grow passed the initial awkwardness of intimacy, they go on to establish a higher level of desire and enjoyment, and so the frequency of intercourse becomes incredibly regular.

For every married couple, this is the most cherished phase of intimacy; it is the stage where each other's bodies no longer seem unfamiliar, but instead become beautifully cherished places that your every sense wishes to explore.

There should be no greater satisfaction for a man than knowing that his demonstration of love; this act of sex, is enjoyed fully and deeply by his wife, and every woman's want for intimacy increases from simply knowing that her husband is captivated by her physically.

The honeymoon phase serves as an exploration for both husband and wife in understanding these elements of one another; it is a time when you should feel most at ease about discussing the boundaries of your sexual interactions.

This is where communication is a key to attaining the healthiest marital discourses.

How and when we choose to communicate our sexual preferences will heavily bear upon the outcome of the conversation. There will never be any success achieved if a man chooses to address his wife's lack of desire at a time when she has just finished cooking dinner and has just sat down after putting the children to bed, or if a woman chooses to voice her dissatisfaction at the end of an act of intimacy.

A marriage is based upon respect – this respect starts with how we communicate our concerns to one another. Naturally, if either partner is unhappy, then there needs to be time set aside in order to speak honestly, but respectfully with one another.

Some basic tips on how to communicate what you want would be through subtle, flirtatious conversation; this can be face-to-face, or via message or telephone calls.

1. Tell them what works for you.

For example, as you wind down with your spouse at night, snuggle up on the couch, and use these opportunities to sincerely thank them for something nice that they may have done for you that day; this conversation opener will immediately soften them to you. As you remain physically close, use that moment to increase skin-to-skin touch – you will see a reciprocation of this from your spouse. As this naturally escalates, tell your spouse what creates enjoyment for you; something as simple as *"I love it when you stroke my hair"* or *"I love it when you kiss my neck"*. In this state of closeness, when you use encouraging language to share what you enjoy, you will see that your spouse will seek to increase upon that act in order to see your enjoyment escalate.

2. Don't be afraid to say what you feel.

We are very aware of the fact that we have certain desires and fantasies that we may wish to explore with our partner however, vocalising these can seem almost impossible. There is always a way.

If you feel too shy to say it to your partner for fear of what they may respond with, use other means. Leave a note, or a send a text, but word it so that it speaks of how much you love your partner, and how you hope to increase that love through your intimacy. You are one another's confidants; to be able to be vulnerable and know that your needs are being heard and handled with care, will naturally cause an increase in your closeness.

It should also be noted that any partner receiving such notes or messages from their spouse should not demean them, nor dismiss them. Put yourselves in your spouse's shoes; imagine for a moment their fragility in opening up to you in this manner – show them a loving response, and use this as a means to share concerns with affection and respect.

3. Talk the talk, and walk the walk.

Another great way to open the conversation is by asking your partner how *you* can perform better for *them* when it comes to intimacy. It is such a shared act of love that *needs* both partners to be open to the want of the other.

By asking your spouse what they want from you, this almost automatically opens them to asking what you want from them.

Be prepared to put your partner's needs into action; the most damaging thing that you can do is to hear their plea, and then dishonour it by simply dismissing it, whilst remaining fulfilled yourself.

When we start applying these simple tips into the early stages of our marriage, in'shaa'Allah, we will see the blossoming of a beautiful rapport between husband and wife; each partner wishes to give, and gain satisfaction undoubtedly, a healthy intimate relationship blooms.

THE ROUTINE YEARS:

Many of us may be in a marital situation where the honeymoon phase has long left us, and we have been married a number of years, with a few children in tow.

Typically, at this stage of marriage the primary complaint that I hear from couples is that sex is almost non-existent, or is something that very few women feel that they have the time for, leaving the menfolk rather frustrated in this respect.

The above, is very much a generalisation that I am drawing based upon my own interactions with couples; that is not to say that this is the norm for everyone. Ma'shaa'Allah, there are those couples who have managed to successfully retain healthy intimacy throughout their married lives, and long may their happiness last.

The secrets to such success boils down to recognising the routine in your life, and then BREAKING IT!

Yes, you heard me! Break the routine. Change the situation that you find yourselves monotonously following.

If you know that your marriage falls into this criteria, take a moment just now, think about your spouse, ask yourself what do you love about them? Which aspect of their person makes you instantly smile? Hold that thought. Imprint it in your mind. Next time you see your partner – tell them:

"You know, I was just thinking about you...."

That statement in itself is so deep. It serves multiple purposes, firstly, it reminds your partner that you still think about them, that they are someone who still holds a significant part of your daily thoughts, secondly, by telling your spouse that when you think of them, you are thinking about their positive aspects, this serves to remind them that you value them and you see the goodness that they bring, and lastly, by telling your spouse that they can still make you smile serves as a means of sharing happiness, Alhamdulillah.

It is such a simple act that just opens the way to a happier rapport between a husband and wife who may simply have fallen into a co-existent setup.

This initial action is just the first step of many that are needed to heal a relationship that has moved into routine, use it to begin communicating change.

For example, men, when you see your wives struggling with the kids and getting the dinner on, why not take the initiative, and help her with one of the tasks; by helping her, even when you may be tired after a day's work, shows that you care for her, and it also means that the work gets done faster, therefore leaving more time for you as a couple at the end of a night.

In addition, women, do not shy away from asking friends or family to look after the kids for a few hours every few weeks or so, and make some time for yourself to dress up and have a much-needed date night with your husband.

The sad reality of this phase is that each partner just accepts that this will be as good as it gets, but what seems to have been forgotten is that once upon a time, things were better than this.

This is a reminder for all who are in this phase, your marriage and its health is within your hands – if you wish to remain in "acceptance" then that's fine, but if you want things to change, then you need to *be that change.*

Reminisce with your partner and work hard on reigniting the love that was once there.

In conclusion, sex matters. We must understand that intimacy is a foundational aspect of marriage. For those amongst us who have dismissed sex as a lesser issue in marriage, they have misunderstood the importance of this bond, and the manner in which it serves to strengthen the relationship between husband and wife. To end, it's important to emphasise that no external factor or source should determine how intimacy should be with your spouse, this is something that the two individuals must seek to explore and achieve amongst themselves.

Life Lesson 7:

"Intimacy grows from the seeds of trust and communication. Nurture those seeds and you will find your relationship in a healthier state."

CHAPTER 11: So, What Next?

As we have journeyed through our analysis of these 7 Myths of Marriage™, you may have come to appreciate the common thread that seems to embody each of these; love, communication, trust and intimacy.

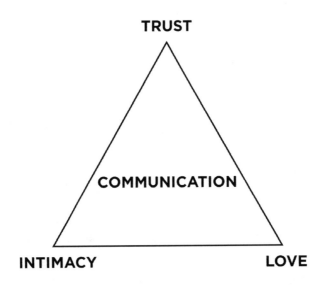

The above diagram demonstrates how these factors are essentially interlinked. Trust forms the peak of a relationship; where it is optimal, a relationship is known to thrive and grow healthily. Naturally as trust grows, we come to find that the love and/or respect between partners begins to naturally increase. There is a greater understanding of one another's needs, and greater desire to fulfil these. As trust and love build up, the cycle naturally develops an increased momentum that pushes towards more healthy intimacy. This cycle continues to feed itself as we tend to find that where there is healthy intimacy in a marriage, there is deep sense of trust and love.

At the heart of all of this lies communication. It is the most central aspect to a healthy marriage. Where a husband and wife can communicate effectively, a relationship will expand in ways that it cannot with any of the external factors alone. Essentially, love, trust and intimacy depend on the existence of communication in order to thrive in a marriage. It is only through verbal and non-verbal communication that a spouse learns to trust their partner; it is primarily through our communication that we express our love for our spouse, and shed any misunderstandings that may arise, and it is based upon healthy dialogue that spouses learn the means by which to fulfil one another's sexual needs.

So we see, in order to dispel myths in marriage, we must learn the art of communication, and this is something that we all have the means to refine, no matter which stage we might find ourselves to be in.

Even prior to embarking on the path of marriage communication factors in; we need to know what our personal needs are, and how to express these to our parents and potential suitors. We need to learn the art of honesty – something that we must exercise upon ourselves first and foremost.

As a marriage progresses, naturally it will be faced with life's many challenges, and in order for these challenges to be dealt with accordingly, a husband and wife must know how to share their anxieties and stresses effectively, without devaluing the other's feelings in any way.

It may seem so basic, but it is so completely profound. I know of one particular individual who has suffered three failed marriages; he was never sure of what was going wrong. In his first marriage, he followed a desire-filled whim, only to learn that there was such disparity in his and his wife's character. In his second marriage, he came to find someone who seemed to have a more level understanding however, her character was condescending and domineering, and as a result, ultimately it led to failure. Lastly, he found obedience and humility, but a complete blank with understanding and communication; the relationship very quickly began to feel hollow as there was no substance. When he spoke with me about his past distresses, I immediately saw the flow chart come to mind. Each of his marriages had one or more of the external factors: the first had love and intimacy, but failed to develop any trust, and most definitely lacked communication. The second had intimacy and trust, yet lacked warmth and love, therefore communication was something that withered due to lack of nourishment. The last was filled with love, trust and steadily increasing intimacy, but the complete lack of communication caused a hollowness to become apparent, and led to an eventual corrosive crumbling of the marriage. When I highlighted this to him, he was taken aback; in that moment, he was struck by realisation – he had neglected communication as being a vital factor in developing his marriages – he had never focused on truly nurturing this. He, like so many of us, believed that the five minute superficial "conversation" at some stage during the day was deemed sufficient in keeping a marriage growing.

In reality, your spouse should be your greatest protector; they should be the one person in whose hands you can place your greatest fears and anxieties, and know they will not be used to destroy you, they will be held tight and hidden so as to protect you from harm. Your spouse should ultimately be your best friend; that one person that you instantly need to share the most mundane to the most thrilling activity in your day.

EVERY MARRIAGE HAS HOPE:

Using the earlier flow chart, each individual can assess which element is weak within their marriage, and then focus the attention to the relevant area as appropriate, much of which was explored in earlier chapters. I would however like to elaborate a little further on the heart of the flow chart; communication, as I genuinely see this as the lifeline of every relationship.

HOW TO IMPROVE COMMUNICATION:

For those of you yet to marry begin to understand how you communicate, and how you understand and process situations; once you have a greater sense of your own understanding, you are immediately better equipped to deal with those around you.

For those of you who are married the process requires some self-reflection; when was the last time you and your spouse had a conversation about your relationship? When did you last discuss how happy/unhappy you are within the relationship? When was the last time you were truly honest about your feelings about the things that matter? The frequency of such conversations will be an immediate litmus test for the health of your marital communication.

If things are regular for you then ma'shaa'Allah, keep doing what you are doing but for those of you have come to realise that there seems to be a gaping hole, do not fear – there is still hope.

Re-establishing communication that has been lost takes time and patience. Firstly, we need to begin with ourselves; when we are engaged in conversation, do we listen attentively, or do we find ourselves listening half-heartedly? In addition, does our listening comprise of us being empathetic, or do we listen merely to make our own points in retort to our partner?

The most fundamental aim of communication is seeking to understand the other party, whereas it would seem, more often than not, we communicate with others by seeking to impose our understandings upon them. This is something that needs to be reflected upon, and can be altered quite simply by forcing ourselves to pause when we wish to speak up in conversation, and to take that brief moment to establish whether what we wish to say is of benefit to the person listening.

In essence, we are forcing ourselves to empathise; we are placing ourselves in the shoes of others and questioning whether we would tolerate that form of communication if we were to be met with it. There is truly no greater sign of love, respect and trust than communication which is embodied with empathy; it is a means of saying "I am here with you on this journey" and it is such a deep way in which to strengthen a marital bond.

Look upon the pyramid of marriage and establish which element is weak in your relationship, and know that today is your day to introduce mending into your marriage.

CONCLUSION:

Marriage is the most blessed gift that we will ever come to find in our lives, if we learn the art of working effectively within it.

In an era where we are exposed to innumerable distractions it becomes difficult to prioritise our time and our efforts appropriately. Anything that holds significance in our lives must be honoured with our undivided attention.

From this moment onwards, I want you to make that promise to yourself; promise that you will seek to respect your spouse with quality time, and enhanced communication, you will seek to remind yourself of their beauty when you both become lost in flaws, you will learn their language of love because you know that you wish to take their hand, and walk together in life, and in your Hereafter.

Today is your first step towards a happier marriage, and a happier self. Begin with that promise, and go forth with the tools within this book.

"The longer we look upon others with our souls, the more beauty we come to find."

Abu Layth

Glossary

In'shaa'Allah	If Allah Wills
Ma'shaa'Allah	What Allah Willed
Alhamdulillah	All Praise is to Allah
Deen	Faith
SubhanAllah	Glorified is Allah, Perfect is He
Subhanhu wa ta'ala	Glorified, the Most High
Sallallahu alayhi wasallam	Peace and blessings be upon him
s.a.w	Peace and blessings be upon him
RadyAllahu anha/anhu	Allah being Pleased with her/him

Acknowledgements

Indeed, all praise is due to Allah, we praise Him and seek His Help and forgiveness. We seek refuge in Allah from our souls' evils and our wrong doings. He whom Allah guides, no one can misguide; and he whom He misguides, no one can guide.

I bear witness that there is no god except Allah alone without any partners. And I bear witness that Muhammad is His servant and Messenger.

It is by His Infinite Mercy that I find myself in this wonderfully exciting chapter of my life, a chapter that I never believed would become my reality, and so I begin my book with a reminder that is so profoundly apt to the context of my life:

"Life consists of two days, one for you and one against you.
So when it is for you, don't be proud and reckless, and when
it's against you, be patient, for both days are a test for you."
Ali ibn Abu Talib   (radyAllahu anhu)

I pray this book brings you as much benefit as I have gained from writing it.

I would like to take this opportunity to acknowledge a few wonderful people, without whom none of this could have been possible.

Firstly, my darling Mother; your absence will always be felt, but in it, I have found the strength and desire to be better, in order that I may honour you eternally, in'shaa'Allah. My dear Father, through the blessing of your presence, I continue to have the love and support that is unwavering; I hope that I am able to make you proud of me as your son.

Secondly, my wife, children, siblings and friends, each of you have shown patience beyond measure, and give me reason to continue on such endeavours.

Lastly, a few special individuals who have inspired me through their own work or through personal efforts in assisting me, I am forever obliged to you all; Sh Muhammad AlShareef, Founder of AlMaghrib Institute and DiscoverU, Sh Abdul Hakim Quick, Brendon Burchard, Tony Robbins, Jiva Akbor, and Sabira Ali.

And to each and every one of you who has believed in my work, and followed me ardently, may Allah bless you for the impact that you have had upon my journey; may any good that comes of my efforts be apportioned to each of you, by Allah's Infinite Mercy. Ameen.

I am endlessly grateful to My Creator, for allowing me this opportunity, and I cannot thank you, my dear readers enough for consistently showing me your love and respect through embracing my projects.

Remember folks, Live to Inspire! ™

About the Author

Born in Wales, and brought up in Scotland, Abu Layth has been an adventurer from his early days.

Having experienced the heights of Everest, and delved into the depths of Ocean Rescue, Abu Layth was always seeking new challenges. The real game-changer came in the form of inspiration from some of our era's great figures in personal development, including Muhammad Alshareef, Brendon Burchard and Tony Robbins. It was only then that Abu Layth endeavoured upon his greatest challenge to date; his LifeLessons series.

Through an ever-growing social media presence Abu Layth went onto pen his first written piece; *7 Life Lessons: Overcoming Your Past Self* ™. This was so warmly received across the globe that it ignited Abu Layth's passion for writing, resulting in this highly acclaimed work, seeking to see marriages return to the celebrated status that they were once known to have.

Made in the USA
Charleston, SC
05 June 2016